The Wa the Cross

Meditations on the Death of Jesus

by Katharine Smith

Illustrated by George Boxley

A Redemptorist Publication

Published by Redemptorist Publications
A Registered Charity limited by guarantee.
Registered in England 3261721

Text: Katharine Smith
Illustrations: George Boxley
Layout: Rosemarie Pink

Prayers from *Common Worship: Times and Seasons* are
copyright © The Archbishops' Council 2006

First published in 2007

ISBN-13: 978-0-85231-330-5

Printed by Joseph Ball Limited, Leicester, LE2 5LQ

Alphonsus House Chawton Hampshire GU34 3HQ
Telephone 01420 88222   Fax 01420 88805
rp@rpbooks.co.uk   www.rpbooks.co.uk

About the ...

Author

Katharine Smith grew up in London and is now a Reader at St Andrew's Parish Church in Taunton, Somerset. She is a regular contributor to *Sunday Link* and *Common Worship Living Word* (both published by Redemptorist Publications). Living with her husband and three cats, Katharine also works for a national children's charity and enjoys the American TV drama *The West Wing*, Paul Simon's music and visiting Venice as often as possible.

Illustrator

George Boxley is a multimedia training designer by day. He lives in West London with his wife – a jeweller – and two teenage daughters – one a photographer and one an athlete. Given the chance, he would like to live in New York or Richmond Park, and to play the saxophone a lot better than he does. He is also Katharine's younger brother.

This book may be used in conjunction with
"The Way of the Cross" in
Common Worship: Times and Seasons.

"The Way of the Cross"
Introduction

"In the beginning was the Word, and the Word was with God, and the Word was God. He was in the beginning with God. All things came into being through him, and without him not one thing came into being. What has come into being in him was life, and the life was the light of all people. The light shines in the darkness, and the darkness did not overcome it.

The true light, which enlightens everyone, was coming into the world. He was in the world, and the world came into being through him; yet the world did not know him. He came to what was his own, and his own people did not accept him. But to all who received him, who believed in his name, he gave power to become children of God, who were born, not of blood or of the will of the flesh or of the will of man but of God. And the Word became flesh and lived among us, and we have seen his glory, the glory as of a father's only son, full of grace and truth."

John 1:1-5, 9-14 (NRSV)

These words of St John tell out with joy and excitement good news of glory, grace, truth, light and life. They celebrate the light of the world which cannot be overcome by darkness and the life that is promised to all who believe in the light's power to redeem and save.

Each year, as we tell the story of the last week of Jesus' life, we tell the story of the light of the world shining even in the darkness of fear, hate, injustice and cruelty.

Jesus calls us to be lights in this world. During Lent and Passiontide we can learn from watching and listening to Jesus as he shows what true light looks like in some of the darkest places in this world.

As we tell again the story of our Lord's Passion, it may be that it unfolds to us a little more of the mystery of the suffering and death of our incarnate God, the triumph of his redemptive love and his power to heal us and to bring us to fullness of life as children of God.

This book is not intended to be used in any particular way but these may be helpful suggestions.

The Scripture readings and prayers are taken from "The Way of the Cross" in *Times and Seasons* (published by Church House Publishing and printed with permission) and the meditations are also written to complement this liturgy.

As there are fifteen Bible readings, meditations and prayers it could offer daily readings for individual use from the Second Sunday before Easter, when Passiontide begins, through to Easter Sunday.

Some or all of the Stations could be used in Lent groups or services to introduce a time of meditation and prayer.

However they are used, I hope that these readings, meditations and prayers will open up ways of exploring the events they portray. They are not written to provide answers but rather to raise more questions and to hold those questions in the light of Christ, the light of the world.

It has been a great joy to work with my brother, George Boxley, and I am very grateful to him for his insights, sensitivity and inspirational visual interpretations of these meditations. Thank you, George.

I am also very grateful for the love, encouragement and prayers of my husband, Adrian, my friends, especially Julian Smith and Sue Latimer, and members of the congregation of St Andrew's Church, Taunton – thank you all.

Katharine Smith

1

Jesus in agony in the Garden of Gethsemane
Mark 14:32-36

We watch Jesus, the life and light of the world. We watch him as he faces his final struggle with darkness and death.

He has confronted the darkness and suffering around him; his light and truth have transformed lives held captive to diseases of body, mind and spirit; his compassion, wisdom and energy have captured the imagination of those who met him. His light has shone in the darkness of all who reached out to him in faith, and their darkness has not been able to overcome that light.

Now, his own life-light is threatened as despair and fear close in around him. Now he himself knows the agony of loneliness and the powerlessness of a human being facing unspeakable suffering and death without hope of reprieve.

We know as we follow Jesus on his journey to death that not even that final darkness will overcome this light of the world. If we did not know that, would we be able to watch with him now? Would we not also be overcome with emotion and despairing fear as his friends are? We watch from the other side of the cross, in resurrection light, and in the strength of that light we stay with the reality of his fear and his begging to be spared what is to come.

He faces cruelty and humiliation from within his darkness so that he can stay with us, whatever we face in our own darkness. He knows the cold fear that grips heart and mind; he knows what it is to face certain suffering and death. He knows the extremes of a grief that sweats blood.

In the life of Jesus shines the light of the world and even at its deepest and most terrifying the darkness will not overcome his light.

Lord Jesus, you entered the garden of fear
and faced the agony of your impending death:
be with those who share that agony
and face death unwillingly this day.
You shared our fear
and knew the weakness of our humanity:
give strength and hope to the dispirited
and despairing.
To you, Jesus, who sweated blood,
be honour and glory with the Father
and the Holy Spirit,
now and for ever. Amen.

2

Jesus betrayed by Judas
and arrested
Mark 14:43-46

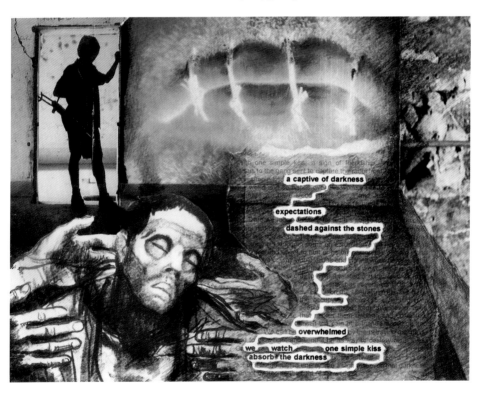

a captive of darkness

expectations

dashed against the stones

overwhelmed

we can watch   one simple kiss
absorb the darkness

With one simple kiss, a sign of friendship, Judas identifies Jesus to the gang sent to capture the rabbi from Nazareth.

With one simple kiss, a captive of darkness identifies the light of the world and so hands over the world's life to certain death.

Perhaps we have stood where Jesus and Judas now stand.

Like Judas, we've felt betrayed by the failure of friends or family to meet our expectations, or to be who we wanted them to be. Dare we judge Judas if he felt his hopes for the triumph of Israel had been dashed against the stones of the Temple? Dare we accuse him if he took drastic action to force Jesus into declaring his kingdom come on earth? Have we never acted in bitterness and anger to hurt or betray someone we loved? And Judas must still have loved Jesus, or why would he end his life when he sees what his betrayal has unleashed?

Like Jesus, we've felt the pain of offering love freely only to have it twisted and thrown back at us in scorn and bitterness.

Jesus has seen conflicts within communities and families: a brother betraying his family by collecting taxes for the occupying forces; sons fighting over inherited land, and people separated from their loved ones because of disease that makes them unclean and unwanted. Now he knows for himself the pain of a friend's desertion and betrayal.

We can be overwhelmed by the betraying darkness, add to its weight and send it on its way to destroy other lives. Or we can watch Jesus. In one simple kiss Jesus accepts and absorbs the darkness; he transforms it, redeeming the act of a friend turned enemy into a sign that even that darkness cannot overcome the light of the world.

Lord Jesus, you were betrayed
by the kiss of a friend:
be with those who are betrayed and slandered
and falsely accused.
You knew the experience of having your love
thrown back in your face for mere silver:
be with families which are torn apart
by mistrust or temptation.
To you, Jesus, who offered your face
to your betrayer,
be honour and glory with the Father
and the Holy Spirit,
now and for ever. Amen.

3

Jesus condemned by
the Sanhedrin
Mark 14:55-64

They already know their judgement and the penalty they wish to impose on Jesus. Now, to produce evidence to justify this, the words and actions of Jesus are taken out of context and twisted. The truth is denied even when it is clearly spoken.

Suddenly, out of the confusion and cacophony of noise comes silence, all eyes on Jesus, a commanding figure amidst this chaos.

"Are you the Messiah?"

The question hangs in the air.

"I AM."

The answer slices through the clouds of prejudice and hatred, and hard-set hearts and minds catch a glimpse of what might be. It is only for an instant, then the moment is gone, the choice made, the sentence passed. He has condemned himself by his own words, truth though they be.

Men and women are still unjustly accused and judged, oppressed and persecuted because of the truth they speak. They speak the truth of who they are, human beings equal before a higher power, but stripped of dignity and human rights by authorities who have set themselves up over all who oppose them. They speak the truth of what they believe, claiming a freedom denied them, and refusing to collude with tyranny and falsehood.

Wherever we are, from small offices to powerful courts of nations, whenever we speak the truth, the one who is truth stands alongside us. In his presence is the promise of the final triumph of truth and justice over lies and oppression. It is with faith in that great truth that we find courage to speak out, believing that, in the end, we will be heard.

Lord Jesus, you were the victim of religious bigotry:

be with those who are persecuted by small-minded authority.

You faced the condemnation of fearful hearts:

deepen the understanding of those who shut themselves off

from the experience and wisdom of others.

To you, Jesus, unjustly judged victim,

be honour and glory with the Father and the Holy Spirit,

now and for ever. Amen.

4

Peter denies Jesus
Mark 14:72

We see Peter's anguish but we also know his future. We know that, on the seashore, Jesus will forgive him and restore him to a new life. He will be transformed into a man of courage and total dedication.

Tonight, though, for Peter the light of his world is extinguished. He's alone and afraid. He saw the hurt in his Lord's eyes and knows that his denial has brought more grief into the heart of a man who only loved and served his followers.

Nothing will comfort Peter. He knows only fear, shame, guilt and self-hatred, and no one could judge and condemn him more than he does himself.

It's hard to watch Peter, to hear his denial and witness his tears. It's hard because we know only too well that sense of failure and shame at our lack of courage. Too often, we act out a denial of knowing Jesus when we behave in selfish, resentful and defensive ways to protect ourselves from condemnation or ridicule.

Peter followed Jesus as far as his human strength and courage would take him. Some of us might not have gone as far as the High Priest's courtyard. But with our vision enlightened by the resurrection we see more of Peter's story and it reveals the way our story might unfold.

Like Peter, we will learn that in our own strength we can only go so far in faith. Like Peter, we will learn to accept our failures and limitations so that we can be healed, restored and forgiven through the grace of God in Christ.

Like Peter, we will come to understand that Jesus, the light of our life, can and will lead us out of the prison of guilt and self-hatred to start again in the freedom of grace and truth.

Lord Jesus, as Peter betrayed you,
you experienced the double agony
of love rejected and friendship denied:
be with those who know no friends
and are rejected by society.
You understood the fear within Peter:
help us to understand the anxieties
of those who fear for their future.
To you, Jesus, who gazed with sadness
at his lost friend,
be honour and glory with the Father
and the Holy Spirit,
now and for ever. Amen.

5

Jesus judged by Pilate
Mark 15:14-15

There is silence. All eyes are on Jesus, a compelling figure at the centre of this coming together of Jewish and Roman authority.

"Are you the King of the Jews?"

The question hangs in the air, so much depending on the reply.

"You say so."

Like thunder rolling around a threatening sky, accusation after accusation is hurled at the innocent one.

A vision, like a splinter of light, cuts through Pilate's confusion, political cynicism and fear for his own position. He sees a glimpse of a world far removed from the one he knows. In his mind, he searches for a way forward: a way that will release an innocent man, appease these vociferous religious rulers and safeguard the power of Rome. He seizes the opportunity that presents itself in Barabbas and makes his offer to the crowd, who reject it with all the anger and hatred they can muster.

The moment is gone and Pilate loses sight of that other world: his choice is made, the strange alliance between oppressor and oppressed is forged as Pilate hands Jesus over to torture and death.

Today we are still unjustly accusing, judging and oppressing others because we cannot allow truth and justice to lighten our darkness. We deny the equality of all people, we refuse freedom of speech and tolerance of beliefs not our own. We twist all we see and hear to justify our own self-interests.

Whenever we deny and quash truth, the one who is truth stands before us, waiting, loving and believing that somehow, in the end, we will hear him and allow his presence to transform the darkness of injustice with his merciful light and life.

Lord Jesus, you were condemned to death
for political expediency:
be with those who are imprisoned
for the convenience of the powerful.
You were the victim of unbridled injustice:
change the minds and motivations
of oppressors and exploiters
to your way of peace.
To you, Jesus, innocent though condemned,
be honour and glory with the Father
and the Holy Spirit,
now and for ever. Amen.

6

Jesus scourged and crowned with thorns
Mark 15:17-19

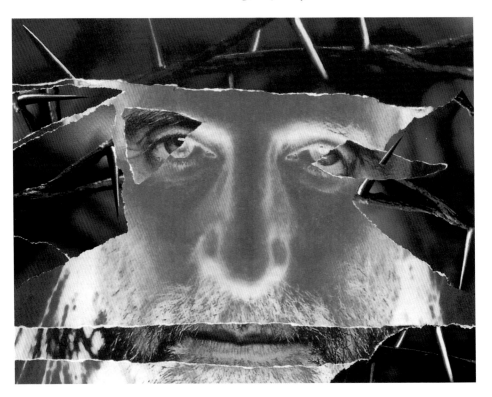

"What it is to be soldiers of the great Roman empire! We can flog a man almost to death and then when he's bleeding, nearly senseless and totally powerless, we taunt him and mock him and abuse his humanity. We can do it because we are so great and powerful and strong!

"I'm not squeamish. I can prove myself in battle as well as any man. I can stand against an enemy who's worthy of the fight. But this Jesus was no threat to the authority of Rome. I've heard him teaching, watched him healing and wondered whether he might be right about God and love.

"They said he was an impostor, a self-proclaimed Messiah who had to be silenced once and for all. They're making us do the dirty work of execution, but I think they're wrong. As he reels from the blows, his blood, sweat and tears mask the life and light I once saw in his eyes, and when those tortured eyes meet mine I see in them only honesty and integrity. I have to look away.

"The scourging is done, his skin flayed to the very bone. Let him go, let him find relief for his pain. This should be the end of it. But it's not. Now we have to crucify him, if he lives long enough.

"I don't know what we're doing. I do know there are people here who will live to regret this day.

"Jesus, don't look at me in that way. Maybe you were right in what you said. But it's too late now. You're as good as dead and there's nothing I can do. I have orders to follow. The kingdom of your God, in the end, has no power and we are the great Roman empire!"

Lord Jesus, you faced the torment of barbaric
  punishment
and mocking tongue:
be with those who cry out in physical agony
and emotional distress.
You endured unbearable abuse:
be with those who face torture
and mockery in our world today.
To you, Jesus, the king crowned with thorns,
be honour and glory with the Father
and the Holy Spirit,
now and for ever. Amen.

7

Jesus carries the cross
Mark 15:20

Jesus sets out on the final stage of his journey to the cross, already exhausted and in a physical agony almost unbearable to watch. They lead him out into the streets of Jerusalem where life is going on as normal for most people. But we watch only him.

He has been wrongly accused and condemned, mocked and humiliated, but there is deeper pain and fear tormenting him at the ending of his life among those he came to save.

He carries the sorrow of a lover who has been rejected; a healer whose gift has not been accepted; a messenger of peace who has been met with hatred and anger.

He carries the loneliness of a loving teacher who has been misunderstood; a faithful and selfless friend who has been betrayed and deserted.

He is a messenger of God, but fears the message has gone unheard; a servant of God, but fears he may not have done enough; a Son of God, but fears the darkness brooding over his soul; a son of man who fears his approaching death.

We can see the sorrow, the longing, the fear and the loneliness that go beyond human understanding. As Jesus struggles with the weight of the cross and the torment in his mind, we pray that somehow, deep in his darkness, a flickering light of hope still burns for these final hours.

We know, Lord, that the road you are now treading, though it leads to your death, is the road to our salvation. We watch and with thanksgiving we pray.

Lord Jesus, you carried the cross
through the rough streets of Jerusalem:
be with those who are loaded
with burdens beyond their strength.
You bore the weight of our sins
when you carried the cross:
help us to realise the extent
and the cost of your love for us.
To you, Jesus, bearing a cross not your own,
be honour and glory with the Father
and the Holy Spirit,
now and for ever. Amen.

8

Simon of Cyrene helps Jesus to carry the cross
Mark 15:21

that's how it is when you follow him

"It started like any other day in Jerusalem at a festival: crowded streets, noise, pungent smells and an atmosphere of tension between people of Israel and soldiers of Rome.

"There was a crowd following three men condemned to crucifixion. The sight sickened me and I tried to push past to get away from the scene. Suddenly, I was grabbed by a soldier and ordered to help one of the convicts carry his cross. I protested – why should I help such a man? Then he looked into my eyes. He appeared to be more than half dead, ready to collapse with exhaustion, but he gave me the faintest of smiles.

"I can't remember if he actually said the words 'Simon, follow me', but somehow I heard them. They seemed to come from far away and long ago. I heard the voice and saw the smile before it was contorted with pain. I felt the breeze coming off the water, the turning of the tide, and the certain knowledge that life would never be the same. I lost all thought for anything else and took up his cross.

"I did what I could to ease his burden. I wish I could have eased the burden he seemed to carry in his heart. Yet when I came away I felt as if somehow he had eased the burdens in my heart.

"That's how it is when you follow him. Serving him and allowing him to serve you is part of the mystery of love and redemption. You can't grasp this without living it, but it's not easy, it's costly. It cost Jesus everything, even life itself. When my memory feels again the weight of his cross on my shoulder, I wonder at the strength of the love that revealed this great truth."

Lord Jesus, you were worn down by fatigue:
be with those from whom life drains all energy.
You needed the help of a passing stranger:
give us the humility to receive aid from others.
To you, Jesus, weighed down with exhaustion
and in need of help,
be honour and glory with the Father
and the Holy Spirit,
now and for ever. Amen.

9

Jesus meets the women of Jerusalem
Luke 23:27-31

The women of Jerusalem are still weeping, with women across the world. They mourn the loss of husband, father, son and brother whose lives have been taken in conflict or by terrorism. They weep for those who have used their own bodies to bring a devastating end to the lives of others. Some weep in poverty, fear and oppression. Some weep in relative safety and wealth, but while such hatred and prejudice remain unleashed, everyone is in danger: security is an illusion, and our fragile lives are too easily hurled into what seems like oblivion for any of us to be complacent.

The plight of one innocent young man being paraded through the city streets towards death attracts little attention. He is one of many who are thus ill-treated and we can no longer bear the scale of suffering such as this.

His plight takes on overwhelming significance when it's seen as an act of reconciling love and sacrifice.

The road he treads is one of love, self-giving, acceptance and forgiveness. It leads to death, but beyond that it leads to new and everlasting life.

When the world becomes so unbearable that we cry for mountains to fall on us and for darkness to cover us, but the road he treads offers healing, peace and salvation, how long will we delay before we follow him?

Lord Jesus, the women of Jerusalem wept for you:
move us to tears at the plight of the broken in our
   world.
You embraced the pain of Jerusalem, the "city of
   peace":
bless Jerusalem this day
and lead it to the path of profound peace.
To you, Jesus, the king of peace
who wept for the city of peace,
be honour and glory with the Father
and the Holy Spirit,
now and for ever. Amen.

10

Jesus is crucified
Mark 15:24

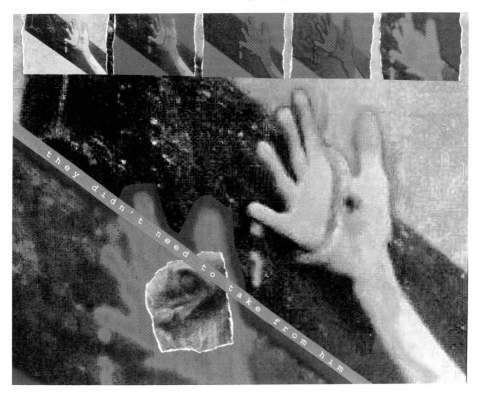

They crucified him. Three stark words to describe an act so brutal and cruel that few can bear to watch it happen. Hammers driving nails through flesh into wood. Blood staining the ground beneath the body. The sound of human agony and the dreadful indifference of the torturers. No wonder the people who tell this story never dwell on this final act. He was crucified, and felt in his body all the physical pain that human beings can deliberately inflict on each other.

They divided his clothes among them. They stripped him, exposed his torn flesh and lifted up his naked body, shaming and humiliating him by turning his final hours into an exhibition for all who pass by.

Turning their backs on the man they had treated as anything but human, they cast lots for his clothes. What sort of trophy is it that is taken off a powerless man when he can do nothing to resist? This is a man who loves his enemy even now and would gladly give his shirt or walk the extra mile. They didn't need to take from him. They had nothing to fear from him.

The wounds now inflicted on Jesus will leave their scars. They are for us signs of the promise that when we are hurt we will be healed; when we are broken we will be made whole; when we are shamed and humiliated we will find dignity restored and, when we suffer the darkness of loneliness and isolation, God's loving presence will surround us.

We will carry the scars, but we will also be transformed and made new in body, mind and spirit within the love of our Lord Jesus Christ.

Lord Jesus, you bled in pain
as the nails were driven into your flesh:
transform through the mystery of your love
the pain of those who suffer.
To you, Jesus, our crucified Lord,
be honour and glory with the Father
and the Holy Spirit,
now and for ever. Amen.

11

Jesus promises the kingdom to the penitent thief

Luke 23:39-43

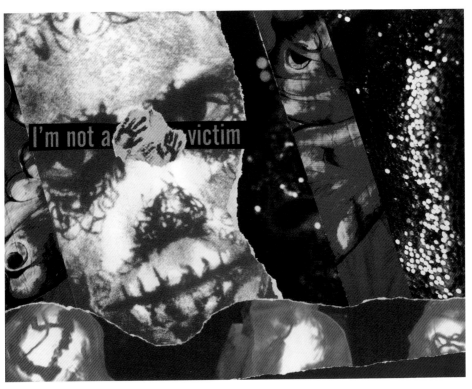

I hear the promise Jesus gives to the penitent thief and wonder at its meaning and the paradox of new life given at the time of death.

I think I might know, a little, how this man feels, nailed to a cross, unable now to undo any of the things that brought him to this desperate point. My cross is not a real one made of rough wood. My cross is the past to which I'm nailed and my pain is in my soul. But I feel something of his despair, of his bitter-tasting regret and icy fear of the darkness that lies ahead.

It's too late now to mend relationships broken by my selfishness and lack of love; to say I'm sorry for the hurt I've caused; to forgive the damage done to me; to quell the fear inside and live a bolder life; to dream the dreams and reach out to grasp them; to value life and live it to the full. It's all too late and I want to leave the darkness of this life for that unknown darkness that surely can't hurt as much.

Then I hear again this story of hope and promise. It's so familiar yet suddenly so compelling, filled with meaning. Like that thief, in Jesus I see my own anguish and despair and know he understands. I know why I'm here but not why he's beside me. I know my own self-loathing, but also now see his flowing compassionate love. It breaks my heart and I cry the words, "Jesus, remember me when you come into your kingdom."

Suddenly I know it's not too late, it's not too late at all. I have been given power to become a child of God. This is only the beginning and there is time.

Lord Jesus, even in your deepest agony
you listened to the crucified thief:
hear us as we unburden to you our deepest fears.
You spoke words of love in your hour of death:
help us to speak words of life to a dying world.
To you, Jesus, who offer hope to the hopeless,
be honour and glory with the Father
and the Holy Spirit, now and for ever. Amen.

12

Jesus on the cross, his mother and his friend
John 19:26-27

A mother should never have to watch her son face a slow and horrible death. Perhaps only those who have suffered in this way can imagine what Mary is experiencing. What other horror is there when that death is inflicted by others?

She stands there with a friend and their grief is terrible. They can do nothing to take away Jesus' pain or end his torment. What light can there be in this darkness which annihilates all that made life worthwhile?

We watch as his mother and his friend do, but we can't see with their eyes, hear with their ears, know with their minds or feel the anguish of their breaking hearts. We haven't lived alongside him, through joy and laughter, through tears and grief, and now towards death. Even if we could reach them, speak to them, tell them that he will live again, would it make their pain and grief any easier to bear?

If they could hear us, maybe we could push back the darkness just a little, enough to restore a seed of faith that it will not, after all, overcome completely.

For as Jesus shows his love for his mother and his friend, we see that there really is nothing, neither death nor life, neither angels nor demons, neither the present nor the future nor any heavenly powers, neither the world above nor the world below, nothing in all creation that can separate us from God's love in Jesus Christ even as he suffers on the cross.

Mary and the disciple reach us and call us to be like them. United by their love of Jesus and called to do so, they care for one another. So, too, we are called to be the Christ-light in each other's darkness.

Lord Jesus, your mother and your dearest friend
stayed with you to the bitter end,
yet even while racked with pain
you ministered to them:
be with all broken families today
and care for those who long for companionship.
You cared for your loved ones
even in your death-throes:
give us a love for one another that is stronger
even than the fear of death.
To you, Jesus, loving in the face of death,
be honour and glory with the Father
and the Holy Spirit,
now and for ever. Amen.

13

Jesus dies on the cross
Mark 15:34-37

Some things stay the same...
Some change dramatically

"Is it nothing to you, all you who pass by?
Look and see if there is any sorrow like my sorrow."

Broken, grieving and forsaken, the heart of the Son of Man is stilled by death, and the pain is felt by the great heart which sustains the life of all creation. For an infinitesimal fraction of a second it is as if the entire universe suffers with the one through whom it came into being.

In that undetectable splinter of time, the darkness believes it has overcome the light it hates. But the truth is that in that splinter all things are made new. Never again can there be any doubt that love, light and life are at the heart of all that is, seen and unseen.

And because love, light and life are at the heart of all that is, we can know that, one day, chaos will give way to patterns of order; apparently random and meaningless events will give way to purpose and design; hatred and violence will give way to the redemption of love and healing.

As Jesus gives one loud desperate cry and breathes his last, we know the truth: on the cross something new is being revealed. So let the cross be for us a symbol of meaning, purpose, love and, above all, new life in the one whose human life was ended by the darkness of our world but whose spirit is the light which enlightens everyone.

"Is it nothing to you, all you who pass by?"

No, Lord, it is everything to us.

On the cross is the new revelation of the reality of your presence in our suffering; and in that revelation we see your glory, the glory of a Father's only Son, full of grace and truth.

Lord Jesus, you died on the cross
and entered the bleakest of all circumstances:
give courage to those who die at the hands of others.
In death you entered into the darkest place of all:
illumine our darkness with your glorious presence.
To you, Jesus, your lifeless body hanging on the tree
    of shame,
be honour and glory with the Father and the Holy
    Spirit, now and for ever. Amen.

14

Jesus laid in the tomb
Mark 15:46

Joseph takes you into his arms, wonder and love in his eyes. Watched by your exhausted, loving mother he cleans the blood from your naked, tired and battered body. He wraps you in strips of cloth and lays you down in a manger, a bed not your own, but welcome and safe.

Another Joseph takes you into his arms, grief and love in his eyes. Watched by your exhausted, loving mother he cleans the blood and dirt from your naked, battered and lifeless body. He wraps you in strips of cloth and lays you down in a tomb, not your own, but welcome after the excruciating pain and public humiliation that have gone before.

Our birth brings us life in an uncertain and ever-changing world. At the beginning we are vulnerable, dependent on others to care for us as we grow and begin to live our lives. Throughout, we remain vulnerable, not knowing when or how our end will be and dependent on others to lay us to rest.

You who are of all things the Alpha and Omega, the beginning and the end, have shared the vulnerability of being human. Between the manger and the tomb you lived your life among us and we beheld your glory, full of grace and truth.

For now your life is ended, your body hidden to rest in darkness.

It has to be so. You could not live among us without being born. Being born, you could not avoid death, and we know now that it is only through death and from the tomb that you could rise to the new life in resurrection light which you offer to all who follow you.

Lord Jesus, Lord of life,
you became as nothing for us:
be with those who feel worthless
and as nothing in the world's eyes.
You were laid in a cold, dark tomb
and hidden from sight:
be with all who suffer and die in secret,
hidden from the eyes of the world.
To you, Jesus, your rigid body imprisoned in a tomb,
be honour and glory with the Father and the Holy
    Spirit,
now and for ever. Amen.

15

Jesus risen from the dead
Mark 16:4-8

if it is true, we can never be the same again

Radiant light and life blaze out from the tomb. The world has never seen a dawn like this, heralding in a new age and a glory that will never be defeated. Resurrection power fills the air with energy, joy and excitement and the whole creation joins in with songs of triumph and praise.

This is beyond anything we've ever known. But alongside the joy and excitement we also feel terror and amazement. We are afraid, but hide what it is we fear: hope dashed to despair, joy drowned in sorrow again, the discovery of new life turned to grieving for what might have been, good news turned back into the same old story of defeat.

We need to hear again the words of the young man: "Do not be alarmed; you are looking for Jesus of Nazareth, who was crucified. He has been raised; he is not here."

Maybe that's what we're afraid of. For if it is true, we can never be the same again, our lives will be changed and suddenly the world and the people around look very different. We need to hear again and again the reassurance, "Do not be afraid" and "I am with you always." Trusting in those words, we might begin to believe that he has been raised, and that truth will fill our hearts, our minds and our spirits so that we can receive the new life that has just burst into our world.

His life is the light of all people. His light shines in the darkness and the darkness did not overcome it. He lived among us and we have seen his glory, full of grace and truth.

Christ is risen indeed. Alleluia.

Lord Jesus, you were dead but now you are alive:
transform the torments of this world's sin
that we may see your radiant glory.
You were raised from death to life:
may the power of your resurrection live in us
that we may be channels of your true life beyond
    measure.
To you, Jesus, who have broken free from the
    bonds of death,
be honour and glory with the Father
and the Holy Spirit, now and for ever. Amen.